My First Book about the Church

Carine Mackenzie

CF

10 9 8 7 6 5 4 3 2 1
© Copyright 2010 Carine Mackenzie
ISBN: 978-1-84550-570-7

Published by Christian Focus Publications,
Geanies House, Fearn,
Ross-shire, IV20 1TW,
Scotland, U.K.

The scripture quotations in this book are based on
the New King James version of the scriptures.

www.christianfocus.com
email:info@christianfocus.com

Cover design by Daniel van Straaten
All illustrations by Diane Mathes

Printed and bound by
Bell and Bain, Glasgow

Mixed Sources
Product group from well-managed
forests and other controlled sources
www.fsc.org Cert no.TT-COC-002769
© 1996 Forest Stewardship Council

Contents

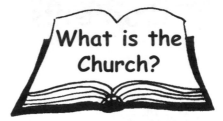

What is the Church?

To the church of God which is in Corinth, to those who are sanctified in Christ Jesus, called to be saints, with all who in every place call on the name of Jesus Christ our Lord (1 Corinthians 1:2).

When God speaks in the Bible about the church, he does not mean a building where services are held. The real church is the people of God, those who belong to him. The church is all over the world, made up of the people everywhere who call on the name of the Lord Jesus.

The church is also the group of people that meet together regularly to worship God.

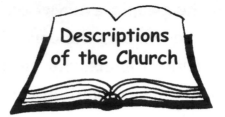

Descriptions
of the Church

Christian

And when he had found him, he brought him to Antioch. So it was that for a whole year they assembled with the church and taught a great many people. And the disciples were first called Christians in Antioch (Acts 11:26).

Christian is one of the names given to those who follow the Lord Jesus Christ - those who are part of the church.

Barnabas and Paul worked with the church in Antioch, preaching and teaching. There the followers of Jesus Christ were first called Christians. Only people who trust in Jesus can be called Christians.

Believers

And believers were increasingly added to the Lord, multitudes of both men and women (Acts 5:14).

A believer is someone who believes the truth about the Lord Jesus Christ. A man once asked Paul, 'What must I do to be saved?' The answer was very simple - 'Believe on the Lord Jesus Christ and you shall be saved.'

God, the Holy Spirit, gives the power to believe. Many people can merely know about Jesus - who he was and what he did.

A true believer will have a personal relationship with Jesus and will put his trust in him.

Faithful

To the saints and faithful brothers in Christ who are in Colosse: Grace to you and peace from God our Father and the Lord Jesus Christ (Colossians 1:2).

When Paul wrote to the church which met at Colosse he called them saints and faithful brothers. They did not just try to do their best to please God; they knew they could not trust their own goodness. They put all their faith and trust in the Lord Jesus Christ. They knew that He had given His life for them.

The Christian who has faith in God, will be faithful to him. God is always faithful to his people, the church.

Without faith it is impossible to please God, for he who comes to God must believe that he is, and that he is a rewarder of those who diligently seek him (Hebrews 11:6).

Family of God

For this reason I bow my knees to the Father of our Lord Jesus Christ, from whom the whole family in heaven and earth is named (Ephesians 3:14-15).

God's people are described as a family. Your family is made up of parents, children, grandparents. You may also have brothers, sisters, aunts, uncles and cousins. Members have a special bond – they belong to each other.

God's people have a special family bond – because they have the same heavenly Father – God. The Lord

Jesus Christ is their elder brother. When Christians meet each other for the first time, they know that they belong to the same family – they are adopted into God's family.

Behold what manner of love the Father has bestowed on us, that we should be called the children of God (1 John 3:1).

Body of Christ

And He put all things under His feet, and gave Him to be head over all things to the church, which is His body, the fullness of Him who fills all in all (Ephesians 1:22-23).

For as the body is one and has many members, but all the members of that one body, being many, are one body, so also is Christ (1 Corinthians 12:12).

Our bodies are made up of many different limbs and organs - all with a different purpose. Our legs and feet are used for walking with. With our eyes we see. We smell with our nose. We work with our hands.

God's church is like a body. Each person is different and useful in his own way.

The Bible tells us that Christ is the Head of this body. Without a head a body cannot live. Without Christ, the church would not survive.

Bride

Husbands, love your wives, just as Christ also loved the church and gave Himself for her (Ephesians 5:25).

A bride and bridegroom love each other so much that they get married and live together as a family.

Jesus Christ is described as the husband who loves his wife, the church, so much that he gave himself for her.

Jesus gave himself for his people, the church when he suffered and died on the cross to take on himself the punishment due for their sins.

There is no greater love than that. 'We love him because he first loved us.' (1 John 4:19)

The church is like the bride who has eyes only for her bridegroom, Jesus Christ. He is the most important person for her.

Building

For we are God's fellow workers; you are God's field, you are God's building (1 Corinthians 3:9).

You also, as living stones, are being built into a spiritual house, a holy priesthood, to offer up spiritual sacrifices acceptable to God through Jesus Christ (1 Peter 2:5).

A house is made up of many stones and bricks all skillfully put together by the builder.

Christians are part of God's spiritual building or house - all joined to Christ who is the chief cornerstone, the most important stone which keeps the building together.

Every stone in the wall of the house is necessary. Every Christian is a necessary part of Christ's church. God is the master builder of this building - the church.

Light of the World

You are the light of the world. A city that is set on a hill cannot be hidden (Matthew 5:14).

A light bulb does not produce light by itself. It only gives light if it is connected to the energy source.

A Christian gives light to the world only by being connected to the Lord Jesus Christ. This light is shown by good deeds. When others see that, they will know it is because Jesus Christ is dwelling in him and they will praise God.

The reflected light in the life of a Christian, will be a help and guide to others, leading them to the great source of light, the Lord Jesus Christ.

For you were once darkness, but now you are light in the Lord. Walk as children of light (Ephesians 5:8).

Sheep

And when he brings out his own sheep, he goes before them; and the sheep follow him, for they know his voice (John 10:4).

The church is described as a flock of sheep, with the Lord Jesus Christ as the good shepherd.

Sheep recognise the voice of their shepherd and follow him to the feeding pastures. He keeps them from danger and looks after them.

The Christian listens to the voice of Jesus the good shepherd. He speaks to him through the Bible.

The Bible gives nourishment and comfort. If he follows the good shepherd he will be protected from harm and danger.

Paul told the elders at Ephesians to 'take care of the flock, over which God the Holy Spirit has made you overseers, to shepherd the church of God, which he purchased with his own blood' (Acts 20:28).

Branches of Righteousness

I am the vine, you are the branches. He who abides in Me, and I in him, bears much fruit; for without Me you can do nothing (John 15:5).

A branch of a tree can only live if it is attached to the trunk whose roots go down into the ground. It will not bear fruit if it is cut off.

The Christian is described by Jesus as a branch of a vine. Jesus himself is the vine. Christians (people belonging to God's church) are the branches. Only through Jesus will the Christian bear fruit and show in his life the fruit of the Spirit - love, joy, peace, patience, kindness, goodness, faithfulness, gentleness and self-control.

God wants his people, the church, to obey his Word.

If you keep my commandments, you will abide in my love (John 15:10).

Blessings given to the Church

Salvation

Nor is there salvation in any other, for there is no other name under heaven given among men by which we must be saved (Acts 4:12).

Jesus saves his church. The name Jesus means Saviour. The Son of God became a man. He was born in this world. He came to suffer and die as a sacrifice for sin - not his own sin (he was perfect) but for the sins of his people, the church. He loves his people so much that he died on the cross so that his people would be saved from the punishment due to them because of their sin.

Those who repent and come to God by faith, receive the great blessing of salvation.

Justification

... being justified freely by His grace through the redemption that is in Christ Jesus ... (Romans 3:24).

Jesus Christ justifies his church. When the Lord Jesus died on the cross for his people, the church, he bought the pardon for all their sins, and made them acceptable in God's sight. God no longer sees their sin, but Christ's goodness. God's people are justified, just as if they had never sinned.

They are no longer condemned by the God who hates sin, but by grace they are accepted as righteous in God's sight.

Therefore having been justified by faith, we have peace with God, through our Lord Jesus Christ (Romans 5:1).

Adoption

Behold what manner of love the Father has bestowed on us, that we should be called children of God! Therefore the world does not know us, because it did not know Him (1 John 3:1).

God adopts his people into his family. God's love is so gracious. Those who trust in his Son, the Lord Jesus Christ, are given the right to become his children. They are adopted into God's family. Jesus Christ is their elder brother.

These children are given a special inheritance from the

Father - everlasting life with him in heaven.

For God so loved the world that he gave his only begotten Son, that whosoever believes in him should not perish but have everlasting life (John 3:16).

Sanctification

To the church of God which is at Corinth, to those who are sanctified in Christ Jesus, called to be saints, with all who in every place call on the name of Jesus Christ our Lord, both theirs and ours (1 Corinthians 1:2).

The church is sanctified by God. God wants his people to be holy like himself. By his grace, his people, the church, learn gradually to hate sin and to stop sinning. They learn also to love and do what is right and holy. God's people are not perfect; they still do say and think what is wrong, but God's work in their heart cleanses them from all sin. Only at death is the Christian perfect. There is no sin in heaven.

Now may the God of peace himself sanctify you completely; and may your whole spirit, soul and body be preserved blameless at the coming of our Lord Jesus Christ (1 Thessalonians 5:23).

Correction

For whom the LORD loves He chastens, and scourges every son whom He receives (Hebrews 12:6).

The church is corrected by God. A father will correct and discipline his child when he does wrong, because he loves him. God will correct and discipline his family too.

His Word, the Bible, will point out error. Sometimes difficult happenings will make us stop and pay heed to God and his will.

Correction is not a punishment, but meant to bring the child back to a loving fellowship with the Father.

No one enjoys discipline, but it is good and a blessing.

No chastening (correction) seems to be joyful for the present, but painful; nevertheless, afterward it yields the peaceable fruit of righteousness to those who have been trained by it (Hebrews 12:11).

What does the
Church do?

Meets Together

... not forsaking the assembling of ourselves together, as is the manner of some, but exhorting one another, and so much the more as you see the Day approaching (Hebrews 10:25).

We can worship God anywhere and even on our own, but it is good for us to meet together. God wants us to worship together with other Christians in the local church group. This makes us stronger and encourages us to live for God. It is good to meet together as often as we can, especially on the Lord's Day.

This gives us fellowship with God's people locally. It also helps us to get to know other believers and to care for each other. This is honouring to God.

Worship

But the hour is coming, and now is, when the true worshipers will worship the Father in spirit and truth; for the Father is seeking such to worship Him. God is Spirit, and those who worship Him must worship in spirit and truth (John 4:23-24).

God is worthy of our worship. He is all-powerful, all-knowing, everywhere, far higher than anything we can imagine. Yet he cares for us. This will make us worship him.

We can worship him by singing or praying, thinking about him or reading, listening about him. We can worship him in church with others, or on our own. We can worship God anywhere.

Oh come, let us worship and bow down! Let us kneel before the Lord our maker (Psalm 95:6).

Pray

Peter was therefore kept in prison, but constant prayer was offered to God for him by the church (Acts 12:5).

When Peter was in prison the church prayed earnestly together for him. God intervened and Peter was miraculously freed from prison. He made his way to the house where the church was meeting. The girl who came to the door to answer his knock could hardly believe her ears.

  She rushed to tell the others. They did not even believe her at first. At last they opened the door and saw Peter. Their prayers had been answered.

Ask and it will be given to you; seek and you will find; knock and it will be opened to you (Matthew 7:7).

Read the Bible

... and that from childhood you have known the Holy Scriptures, which are able to make you wise for salvation through faith which is in Christ Jesus (2 Timothy 3:15).

Search from the book of the LORD, and read: Not one of these shall fail; Not one shall lack her mate.For My mouth has commanded it, and His Spirit has gathered them (Isaiah 34:16).

It is important for God's people to read God's Word, the Bible both on their own and when they meet together with others.

The Bible is the Word of God. It is true. God tells us about himself. He also tells us how he wants us to behave. The Bible gives us teaching and training. It corrects us and warns us against sin. It comforts us in sorrow. It feeds our souls and draws us nearer to Jesus.

And the next Sabbath almost the whole city came together to hear the word of God (Acts 13:44).

Listening and Learning

So then faith comes by hearing, and hearing by the Word of God (Romans 10:17).

We must listen when the Word of God is being read in church or at home. We must listen when a Bible story is being told or when the Bible is being explained by a preacher.

We can learn more and more about God this way. We do not only learn at school. We learn all through life. Grown-ups need to listen and learn about God too.

After Nehemiah had rebuilt the wall of Jerusalem, the people gathered together in an open square and Ezra read the Book of the Law (the part of the Bible that they had), from morning until midday. The ears of all the people were attentive to the Book of the Law (Nehemiah 8:3).

Preaching

How then shall they call on Him in whom they have not believed? And how shall they believe in Him of whom they have not heard? And how shall they hear without a preacher? And how shall they preach unless they are sent? (Romans 10:14-15)

Preach the Word! Be ready in season and out of season. Convince, rebuke, exhort with all longsuffering and teaching (2 Timothy 4:2).

God has chosen some men to be preachers of his Word. A preacher proclaims the Good News about Jesus Christ by explaining what the Bible says. This is called a sermon. The preaching of God's Word is a powerful means of showing people that they are sinners and pointing them to trust in Christ for salvation.

A sermon will give comfort to a Christian, encourage him to be holy and happy in his heart.

Praising

... **speaking to one another in psalms and hymns and spiritual songs, singing and making melody in your heart to the Lord (Ephesians 5:19).**

God's people praise him because he is so great and wonderful. We can worship God by singing psalms and hymns about him and to him. 'Come into his presence with singing,' says Psalm 100. 'I will sing of steadfast love and justice to you, O Lord, I will make music' said David in Psalm 101.

God is pleased to hear his people making a joyful noise to him.

Paul and Silas sang praises to God even when they were in chains in the prison.

After Peter preached on the day of Pentecost, thousands were added to the church. They met together in the temple every day, 'praising God and having favour with all the people' (Acts 2:47).

Offering

So let each one give as he purposes in his heart, not grudgingly or of necessity; for God loves a cheerful giver (2 Corinthians 9:7).

God's people give some of their money for God's work. Money is put in an offering box in church or perhaps a collection is taken during a service.

This money is used to take care of the building, to pay the wages of the people who work in the church. Some may be sent to missionaries or to people in need. This money is actually given to God.

This money should be given cheerfully - not with a grudge or merely out of duty.

Jesus noticed a poor woman putting two small coins into the collection box. Many rich people put in large sums of money.

'She has put in more than the others', Jesus said. 'They all put in out of their abundance, but she out of her poverty, put in all that she had, her whole livelihood' (Mark 12:43-44).

Baptism

Then Peter said to them, 'Repent, and let every one of you be baptized in the name of Jesus Christ for the remission of sins; and you shall receive the gift of the Holy Spirit. For the promise is to you and to your children, and to all who are afar off, as many as the Lord our God will call.' ...Then those who gladly received his word were baptized; and that day about three thousand souls were added to them (Acts 2:38, 39, 41).

Baptism is when water is applied in the name of God the Father, and of God the Son, and of the Holy Spirit. It is an outward sign that demonstrates our need of cleansing by the blood of Jesus Christ and about belonging to the family of God.

Baptism does not cleanse us from sin. Only God can do that. The local church will have a baptism service.

The Lord's Supper

And as they were eating, Jesus took bread, blessed and broke it, and gave it to the disciples and said, 'Take, eat; this is My body.' Then He took the cup, and gave thanks, and gave it to them, saying, 'Drink from it, all of you. For this is My blood of the new covenant, which is shed for many for the remission of sins' (Matthew 26:26-28).

When Christians meet together at church they sometimes have the Lord's Supper. This is also called Communion. Those who love the Lord

Jesus will eat some bread and drink a little wine from a cup. Jesus did this with his disciples before he died. His followers do the same to remember his death. The broken bread is a reminder to us of his body suffering for his people. The poured-out wine reminds us of his blood shed for his people.

Fellowship

And they continued steadfastly in the apostles' doctrine and fellowship, in the breaking of bread, and in prayers (Acts 2:42).

So continuing daily with one accord in the temple, and breaking bread from house to house, they ate their food with gladness and simplicity of heart (Acts 2:46).

People who love the Lord Jesus have a special bond with each other. They enjoy spending time together and talking about the Lord Jesus and the teaching of the Bible.

This special friendship is called fellowship. One of the signs that someone is a Christian is to have love for other Christians.

Church Leaders

Let the elders who rule well be counted worthy of double honour, especially those who labour in the word and doctrine (1 Timothy 5:17).

Every church group has leaders who take decisions about the work of the church.

The pastor and elders help the people to know what the Bible says and to do what is right.

The Bible says that these men must lead godly lives themselves so that they can guide and correct others.

The pastor (or minister) has the added duty of preaching God's Word.

Bearing Fruit

But the fruit of the Spirit is love, joy, peace, longsuffering, kindness, goodness, faithfulness, gentleness, self-control. Against such there is no law (Galatians 5:22-23).

If someone loves the Lord Jesus and is a member of his church, it should be obvious in the way he behaves.

When God the Holy Spirit is working in someone's life, then the fruit of the Spirit is produced. The fruit of the Spirit is love, joy, peace, patience, kindness, goodness, faithfulness, gentleness and self-control.

Witnessing

Then Philip opened his mouth, and beginning at this Scripture, preached Jesus to him (Acts 8:35).

A witness is someone who tells what he has seen or heard. Someone who knows the Lord Jesus needs to tell others about him. Philip told the good news about Jesus to the Ethiopian man he met on the road. He became a believer too.

Living a Christian life is a powerful witness to others who live and work with us. The Christian who has been saved by the Lord Jesus will want to tell others that 'Jesus is Lord'.

Belong to Jesus Christ

... praising God and having favor with all the people. And the Lord added to the church daily those who were being saved (Acts 2:47).

The church belongs to Jesus Christ. He is the one who builds it. Every day people come to trust in Jesus and so become part of the church of Jesus Christ.

The church does not belong to us nor to the minister, but to Jesus because he gave his life for it. He died and rose again to provide forgiveness of sin, salvation and eternal life for his people, the CHURCH.

From the Author

What comes to mind when you hear the word 'church'? Perhaps your child will immediately think of a building with a spire, or a hall where services are held.

When God, in his Word, speaks of the church he is referring to the people who belong to him. They meet from time to time sometimes in a building, but the people are the church.

It is my prayer that the children who use this little book will learn about the church – the privileges and blessings – the responsibilities and work – of those who trust in the Lord Jesus.

He has promised to build his church – he adds to it daily – he cares for it more than we can understand.

CHRISTIAN FOCUS PUBLICATIONS

Christian Focus / Christian Heritage / CF4K / Mentor

Christian Focus Publications publishes books for adults and children under its four main imprints: Christian Focus, Christian Heritage, CF4K and Mentor. Our books reflect that God's word is reliable and Jesus is the way to know him, and live for ever with him.

Our children's publication list includes a Sunday school curriculum that covers pre-school to early teens; puzzle and activity books. We also publish personal and family devotional titles, biographies and inspirational stories that children will love.

If you are looking for quality Bible teaching for children then we have an excellent range of Bible story and age specific theological books.

From pre-school to teenage fiction, we have it covered!

Find us at our web page:
www.christianfocus.com

CF4•K
Because you're never too young to know Jesus